hops—all for thirty-five cents. Americans read books for fun, and saw worlds they understood, in fact recognized. From those of us who spun those carousels to escape to Paris or Maycomb, Alabama, thank you Kurt Brokaw. Those cheap paperbacks, with their intense and glorious covers—painted by wonderful artists—have vanished, but are not forgotten."
—Kent Harrington, author of *Last Ferry Home*

"Kurt Brokaw's publisher recognized that a paperback street vendor could be the best kind of teacher about how books are made available, designed, advertised, and plotted. Word of mouth is the best publicity. An expert conversationalist, Paperback Guy learned on the street the desires and situations that accounted for the popularity of mass-market entertainments in genres such as true crime, mystery, horror, romance, westerns, and sci-fi. Tough guys, rough trade, "women of experience," and mean streets in "blighted" neighborhoods fleshed out the covers and pages. His explanation of Grand Guignol is unique. Great writers like Jim Thompson, David Goodis, and Kurt Vonnegut saw their works in cheap newsstand format flying off the racks. Kurt is their fan, critic, and hype-free salesman.

"Reading Kurt's encounters with some customers (Madonna, Joe Mitchell, Gregory Corso) and paperback writers and illustrators (Philip Roth, Harper Lee, Leo Manso) is as fruitful as reading their bios. Want to see the covers of some of the most notorious pocket-sized titles? Kurt shows dozens—in color! His explanations of why some of his offerings sell are in themselves worth the price of *The Paperback Guy*. So is his story of how he got the respect of the staff of McSorley's Wonderful Saloon.

"Brokaw's book is a New York street-life classic, to be shelved with nonfiction like Friedman's *Tales of Times Square*, Charyn's *Metropolis*, or Broussard's *When Kafka Was the Rage*."
—Jay Gertzman, author of *Pulp According to David Goodis* and *Samuel Roth, Infamous Modernist*

The Paperback Guy

Words from the Sidewalk

Kurt Brokaw

RED BANK   PARIS

2020

The Paperback Guy: Words from the Sidewalk

© 2020 Kurt Brokaw

Kiwai Media, Inc.

kiwaimedia.com

Distributed by Small Press Distribution (Berkeley, California)

spd@spdbooks.org

Book design by Ian Wilcox

Cover photo by Jessica Goldstein

Library of Congress Control Number: 2020930621

Print ISBN: 978-1-037247-06-5

Ebook ISBN: 978-1-037247-09-6

FIRST EDITION

First 99 copies numbered and signed by author.

Introduction

On a brisk fall afternoon one Sunday a few years ago, I walked past a crowded table of magazines and books— pulp fiction—on the east side of Broadway in the heart of Lincoln Center in New York City. Rarely do I pass up the chance to browse used books, and that day was no exception.

With used books, you never know what you'll find. The joy goes deeper too in that you do not even know what you are looking for. The unknown connects by chance with some form of recognition, and the sensation of joy is launched. It's chemical.

The colorful covers of pulp called out and drew me in, and I knew why the genre following Quentin Tarantino's 1994 campy crime film by the same name maintained its power of lassooing its prey. Here were the real items, original paper testimonials to time—manned by a not-all-that-youngish guy with a friendly, boyish face and a worn-out hat. My first thought was Holden Caulfield—as an adult. This would have been the perfect late-in-life scenario for Salinger's adolescent hero. He nodded and watched, sly as a poker player who counted his cards. Which of his book covers would my eyes land on? Would he be able to turn that intel into a sale?

For those who love used books, I don't have to explain how the spirit is lifted when in the presence of good fiction stories that have been told countless times and whose pages have been turned silently in the past by anonymous fingers. The moment gains more zest when you spot an obscure edition penned by a writer prior to her or his cannonization to greatness. If the title was published before the author became famous, book freaks like me in the act of discovery are served an extra rush. Like a bee loading up on pollen, my eyes drank up the well-preserved, artful paperbacks that composed this vintage collection of American literature.

As I recall now combing that table, the memory of my long-time friend and fellow publisher, John Calder, rushed to the top of my mind. John died on August 13, 2018, at the age of ninety-one. In his memoirs he had noted the important trilogy that nourishes the continuity of contemporary writing. The writer and the publisher, Calder wrote, share a sacred link with the bookseller. For it is the bookseller who completes the soulful transfer from writer to reader, and who ingests the beauty and importance of a piece of writing by joining the object with the subject, the book with the reader.

Simply put, literature's mission is completed via the courage and patience of the bookseller.

Meet Kurt Brokaw, the paperback guy, who has been setting up his table of pulp for what he calls "years of Sundays." Kurt intuitively matches and connects what he knows about a book with what he observes or assumes about the reader in front of him. He summed me up to perfection and I walked away that day with a rare copy of Arthur Miller's first novel about anti-Semitism in Brooklyn during World War II.

For $25, I was delighted to acquire an original piece of the American literary landscape and a tiny slice of Kurt's iconic collection, one of the best in the country today. How on earth did he know? And even better, what in fact did he know? That my great-grandfather, Chaim, had first lived on Alabama Street in Brooklyn as a Jewish immigrant sailing from Odessa via Glasgow on the S.S. *Nebraska* in 1891?

When I got home I sent Kurt a small parcel of back copies of the expat literary journal that I had published for two decades from Paris, FRANK.

It struck me that Kurt Brokaw's knowledge of the pulp genre and popular fiction in America should be shared. The relationship between literary history and the format and pricing of books, and the availability of cheap paper and consumer habits, needed to be told, as did the role of painters and graphic artists in the history of publishing. Edgy and marginal tabooed topics were shared with hungry and curious readers via this deceptively complex genre. How pulp fiction fed the supply chain of popular cinematographic hits was an under-reported phenomenon. Kurt's sidewalk table, manned by this knowledgeable chap in an iconic hat, passively held lots of fascinating secrets.

We continued our conversation in the course of a few dozen transatlantic emails, which emerged as this small book.

Pushcart vending in Manhattan traces back to the late 1860s and grew rapidly, with an estimated 20,000 carts crammed primarily into the Lower East Side by 1890. Only a tiny portion of these merchandise carts were selling periodicals, newspapers, pamphlets, or chapbooks, and many of those were in Yiddish and sold at a penny a copy. There is no fee to the City of New York for the vending of written matter. However, "the paperback guy" collects and pays sales tax to New York, included in the price of books sold. He also carries a Certificate of Tax Authority obtained free from the state.

The law that permits the vending of written matter without a license is found in Sections 516-539 of the 1905 City of New York law, which summarizes a number of ordinances passed in the 1890s pertaining to pushcart vending. Section 529 is of special interest, regarding the crying and hawking by vendors before 8:00 a.m., after 9:00 p.m., and on Sundays. Section 535, key to book vending in the 1905 summation, states "Any person hawking, peddling, vending or selling merchandise in the streets of the City of New York shall be deemed to be a peddler, and shall be classified as follows: A peddler using a horse and wagon; a peddler using a push-cart and a peddler carrying merchandise in business; but the selling of newspapers or periodicals in the street is not hereby regulated in any way."

The legality of Kurt Brokaw's rent-free sidewalk status is based on this clause.

—David Applefield, publisher

I can't imagine anyone rich enough or foolish enough to open a rare bookstore in New York City today, so I never did, but I've taken advantage of an 1893 local law that permits the vending of written matter without a license on the sidewalks of New York. To my knowledge New York City is the only city with such a law—it was originally designed to protect Jewish immigrants who peddled chapbooks out of pushcarts in the hurly-burly of Orchard Street for a penny a copy.

People think bookselling is a First Amendment right in the United States. It's not. That amendment essentially says you and I are free to publish most anything we wish. But our method of selling it—how, when, where—is determined by the town, village, or city government. Manhattan has a set of workable rules for book vendors. Though most midtown avenues are frozen, 95 percent of city sidewalks are available. One can occupy a 4'x 8' vending space (about 1.2 meters x 2.5 meters), which must be at least ten feet (about three meters) from a residential door and at least twenty feet (six meters) from a business entrance. A free certificate of tax authority (Tax ID), available through the state, is necessary when vending.

New York's Business Improvement Districts (BIDS) frown on, although legal, all sidewalk vending, because they'd much rather see public sidewalk space licensed and rented to vendors than taken for free. The one true friend I've had up to now in the mayor's chair in New York City was the late Ed Koch, whose grandfather was a street peddler and who once assured me, "as long as I'm in office, you'll never have a problem selling your books." As we sense from the photo, the Lower East Side of Manhattan was far more congested at the turn of the century than the area around Upper Broadway at Lincoln Center where I sell books near the famous Zabar's gourmet food emporium.

Former mayor Mike Bloomberg, presidential candidate and billionaire business and media executive who spent around $160 million of his personal fortune to win elections as mayor of New York City over three terms and twelve years, generally tolerated sidewalk book vending, perhaps because in 2000, before his political runs, he had personally produced an excellent though little-seen movie of his favorite novel, Arthur Miller's *Focus*. His *Focus*, which starred William H. Macy and Laura Dern as a Brooklyn couple experiencing anti-Semitism in 1945, though neither is Jewish, was based on Miller's first book. I've owned and sold a number of copies of the original pulp edition of *Focus*.

Vintage paperbacks from the '40s and '50s, as well as pulp magazines from the '40s and earlier, have always been a hobby and passion. I've spent years patiently explaining to New Yorkers the difference between the true "pulp fiction" from the dozen or so "pulps" I display out of my fifty-year collection and the one hundred or so vintage paperbacks I offer for sale out of thousands I've collected.

This is a good starting point. Pulp fiction magazines and vintage paperbacks are not the same thing. Pulp fiction magazines began around 1895 and enjoyed a half-century run until their New York publishers decided they could make more money selling women's service magazines—at which point magazines, which were published on cheap, ragged-edge-wood pulp paper—whence the genre got its name—vanished and the industry became entirely a glossy and up-market, slick-paper enterprise. "Pulps" had been orphaned alongside "slicks" for the first half of the 20th century. But they had been the starting point for dozens of mainstream writers—Raymond Chandler, Dashiell Hammett, Cornell Woolrich, Leigh Brackett, Ray Bradbury, Arthur C. Clarke, Robert Heinlein, John D. MacDonald, Catherine Moore, Robert E. Howard, and dozens more—who eked out livings writing mostly for a penny a word.

Pulps held at a dime for decades and sold mainly on urban newsstands as well as rough wooden racks in bus stations, pool halls, and army bases. The interesting point is that this mainstream, popular format for American fiction and storytelling ended up being the breeding ground for many of the 20th century's most talented writers, and what was then commercial and marketed as entertainment, we now see is quality fiction and enduring literature. Graham Greene called many of his novels "entertainments." They were that, but thrillers like *Ministry of Fear, Confidential Agent,* and *The Third Man* are timeless works of heft and art.

The point of connection between pulps and paperbacks is the cover art.  Following WWII, pulps began a ten-year slide into extinction, and more and more cover illustrators migrated into mainstream and marginalized paperback houses and began illustrating paperback originals and reprints. That's why so many paperbacks of the era have that "pulp fiction" look—the covers were actually painted by pulp artists. Publishers sensed there was a far wider market for novels at a quarter than for short-story pulp magazines at a dime.

Two of the most familiar pulp stylists of the era were Rudolph (Rudy) Belarski and Earle Bergey. Both were pulp illustrators who bridged easily into paperback illustration. Two of Rudy's prime pieces were *Argosy* and *Cup of Gold*.

In August 1937, *Argosy*—the one mixed-genres pulp—began the first of six parts of *Kingdom Come* by Martin McCall. Rudy's cover shows female and male Nazi brownshirts at the corner of 42nd and Broadway, under an ominous fist—the kind of "early warning signal" pulp editors were alert to, the coming of fascism.

Over a decade later Rudy painted the cover for John Steinbeck's first novel, *Cup of Gold*, first issued in paper in 1950 by Popular Library, a major paperback house. "He sacked Panama for a woman's kisses," pants the breathless cover blurb. The story is positioned as "a swashbuckling tale of adventure and piracy from the author of *The Grapes of Wrath*," which Bantam had released in paper in 1945. Earle Bergey's work follows the same pattern as Belarski's.

The cover of *Startling Stories* is unusual in picturing a "Woman of Wonder"—a kind of precursor to the fictional character Ellen Ripley that Sigourney Weaver created in the *Alien* film series. "Women of Wonder" were smarter and stronger than men in science-fiction and fantasy stories. The first pulp "Woman of Wonder" was probably Pat Savage, the sister of Doc Savage, the pulp superhero created by Lester Dent. Pat was six feet tall and ran a string of high-end dress shops on Park Avenue; she's rarely pictured on Doc Savage covers. But the story, "The Starmen of Llyrdis," by Leigh Brackett, is typical of her vivid, enlightened work; she bridged into movies very early, launching an astonishing career that began with her co-scripting, with William Faulkner, Howard Hawks' *The Big Sleep* and concluded with her writing the screenplay for George Lucas' *The Empire Strikes Back*. Brackett also occasionally partnered with Ray Bradbury in writing pulp stories, and may also have been romantically involved with him.

In 1950 Bergey illustrated the first paper printing of Anita Loos' *Gentlemen Prefer Blondes*. It's a striking cover because glamour gals of the era were often drawn to resemble Lana Turner. Bergey's model looks much closer to Angela Lansbury. The latter actress was building her chops in the '40s, making a lasting impression as a vixen in *Gaslight*. This 1950 cover precedes the movie version of *Gentlemen Prefer Blondes* with Marilyn Monroe.

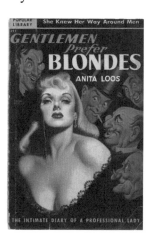

Much of my collection was built sixty years ago off spinner racks in Rexall pharmacies and cigar stores in Iowa and Wisconsin where I grew up and went to college. My dad shot pool on State Street in Dubuque,

Iowa, parking me up front with western and aviation pulps. This is where I learned to read long stories and short novellas, or "novelettes," as they were known. While pulps mostly stayed at ten or fifteen cents through their collective run, paperback books started at a quarter from 1939—when the industry formed itself, much as we still know it today, in just three years.

Compared with hardcover books, most of which were priced at $2 in their primary publishers' editions and forty-nine cents in their reprints by cheaper houses and were mainly sold in department stores, a quarter was a bargain. Around 1952, Signet and other publishers jumped the price on paperbacks to thirty-five cents in order to publish longer novels without abridging them. Signet then went to fifty cents on even thicker novels, using a "double-spine" graphic treatment that suggested you were getting two twenty-five-cent books for your fifty cents. Talk about out-of-the-box marketing. You can see examples in the accompanying photo, along with Signet's "triple-spine" printing (at an unheard-of seventy-five cents) for Ayn Rand's *The Fountainhead* and James Jones' *From Here to Eternity*. Margaret Mitchell's mammoth *Gone With the Wind*, not pictured, didn't make it into mass-market paperback until 1968, at a staggering ninety-five cents.

By 1960 the signs of change were everywhere—the prices, the promotion, the lurid art. Many illustrators stopped reading the novels they were hired to create the covers for because "the specs" were spelled out in an editor's brief. Those tough guys and loose gals with too much past and too little future who had made pulp character classics started to disappear. The shadow of World War II had hung heavy over crime paperbacks until it gradually went away. This roughly matched the demise of *film noir*, both in Hollywood and in France, England, and Mexico, all of which had a strong *noir* presence in the '40s.

My collection is representative of what was sold in that era, meaning a little of everything—classics, hard-boiled crime, science fiction and fantasy, romances, westerns, sports, gay/lesbian, African American literature, film tie-ins, war-related fiction and nonfiction, children's titles. When I lug my books onto the street, I take out about 150 titles, and every author and title offered has a reason for being on display. I've learned that of all the authors of the first half of the 20th century, worldwide, maybe 1 percent are of interest to New Yorkers. I think it would be less outside New York. There is not a living in this.

It's a good thing the overhead stays $1.35 plus $1.35 for bus rides to/from the site, plus $1 for coffee from a sidewalk cart. The most I can lose in a day is $3.70. If I make one sale—which sometimes doesn't happen—I'm ahead of the game.

The challenge, of course, is matching wits with the New York market, which sometimes includes tourists exploring the city from abroad. *Noir*/crime/mystery/suspense leads the parade. The city used to support four excellent used/rare stores specializing in this genre, and now there's only one: Otto Penzler's Mysterious Bookshop. If I could do this in Phoenix, I'd heavy-up the collection with westerns. In Atlanta, I'd put out Faulkner, Tennessee Williams, and Carson McCullers. In London or Paris, I'd try more classics. In most towns or cities I wouldn't even bother, because the interest in vintage paperbacks is almost nonexistent.

Sometimes collectible authors fall into your lap from strange venues. For many years Manhattan had a dive bar just off Fifth Avenue on 23rd Street called Live Bait. It was a construction-worker hangout, kind of a misfit next to Fashionable Fifth. The front window was decorated with fishing gear—netting, tackle boxes, a badly stuffed marlin, rods and reels and lures. There was a hand-lettered sign, IF YOU'RE LOOKING FOR MOM'S COOKING, STAY HOME WITH MOM.

Propped next to a camp stool was a battered copy of *Sucker Bait*, a hardboiled crime novel by Robert O. Saber that had nothing to do with fishing and everything to do with the *femme fatale* on the cover. I 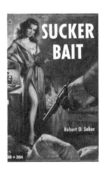 recall slipping the bartender a $10 and his letting me walk out with *Sucker Bait*. Later I learned Saber was actually Milton Ozaki, a Japanese American whose crime novels I was slightly more familiar with. Saber was messier and better suited to a dive bar named Live Bait. The cover of this 1959 Graphic mystery, I'm guessing, was painted by Walter Popp, as he illustrated several other Saber novels published by Graphic.

The two great advantages of being a sidewalk paperback expert are that there's no competition and there's little overhead, though there are plenty of long days I don't make a nickel. The prices on the table start around $15 and work their way up to $1,000. The only authors at or near the high end are Jim Thompson, David Goodis, and Charles Willeford. Several lesbian writers, including Ann Bannon and Marijane Meaker, are approaching that. William Burroughs's *Junkie* and a few other paperback originals like William Faulkner's Armed Services Edition printing of *A Rose For Emily* are in the territory.

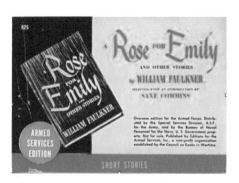

The LA Bantams, a series of titles Bantam unsuccessfully tried in vending machines before concluding paperbacks had no future, are up there. Bantam had been the last major publisher to weigh into the market in 1945, long after the industry had been successfully launched.

There were two dozen titles published by Bantam in 1940, which the publisher attempted to sell via vending machines in Los Angeles. They obviously didn't work well enough for Bantam, which stayed away from mass-market paper publishing until 1945. The Bantam rooster colophon is identifiable by its unkempt plumage, which was trimmed back when Bantam finally entered the mass market-paperback industry in 1945.

In the meantime, in 1939, Pocket launched its first ten titles in test printings in New York City, all of which sold out their runs instantly. Various publishers experimented with vending machines, eager to learn if people would spend a quarter for the same book they'd buy with a dust jacket for $2.00 (mostly) in a legitimate bookstore, or forty-nine cents for the more common hardcover reprints sold mainly in department and stationery stores, and printed on cheaper paper. None of the vending machine attempts panned out, partly because people couldn't pick up and handle this new product, partly because the machines had such limited distribution, and mostly because the covers lacked illustrations. *Tarzan in the Forbidden City* hardly races your pulse when you don't see him "fighting the perils of the place of human sacrifice."

The Charles Boni paperbacks from 1930 were another pre-Pocket experiment. This was a subscription series ($5 a year for a book every month) offered by Charles and Albert Boni, who founded the Modern Library line. The covers and some interior illustrations were by Rockwell Kent—who's certainly collectible—and had handsewn bindings, but the authors and titles were too obscure or esoteric for a mass reading audience. Frank Harris' cowboy memoir would have had the most popular appeal, but other publishers were aware of this experiment and were trying to figure out how to thread the needle between cloth and paper.

For over a year the Argosy bookstore, a fine used/rare shop still going strong here in midtown Manhattan, had over twenty Boni Books sitting in open display on their main floor, in good condition for $10 each. I looked at them and passed on them again and again. The pile just wouldn't go down. No one has ever walked up and requested a Boni title or an LA Bantam.

The rarest items, historically, are 150 copies of a test printing of Pearl Buck's *The Good Earth* sent out to key bookstores and distributors prior to Pocket's 1939 test launch of its first ten titles in New York City. I'm told this test copy of *The Good Earth* was last offered at $7,000.

It has a slightly different arrangement of cover elements than the regular Pocket edition from 1940, which is a $20 book, tops.

I'll never own an original test printing of *The Good Earth*, but among my favorite collectibles are nonfiction accounts of World War II published in the Fighting Forces Series of the *Infantry Journal* imprint. These included several dozen reports from theaters of combat charting U.S. progress. *Soldier Art* includes 215 examples of GI paintings, sculptures, and photographs exhibited in the National Gallery of Art in Washington, D.C., in the summer of '45 with eight pages in full-color letterpress. The Infantry Journal Inc. series had limited distribution on military bases and was given to soldiers, WACs, (the Womens Army Corp), and WAVES, the womens' section of the U.S. Naval Reserves.

The Armed Services Editions (ASE) was a much broader series, encompassing over 1,300 titles, mixing fiction and nonfiction including the *Soldier Art* volume.

Nearly seventy publishers and dozens of printers contributed books and production to the Council on Books in Wartime, a nonprofit organization that was founded during WWII by booksellers, publishers, librarians, and authors in order for books to be used as "weapons in the war of ideas," as they liked to say. The council promoted titles with the clear objective of rallying the American public to maintain the will to win, and to expose the true nature of the enemy. This was the social media campaign of its day. Over 120 million copies were printed in a horizontal format to fit easily in a cargo jacket or pants pocket. Many went abroad and stayed. Some still turn up in rural

European bookshops, worn and tattered, though this visitor didn't find a one in the 4 million books gathered in Hay-On-Wye, the "booktown" between England and Wales.

One extremely desirable ASE title is William Faulkner's *A Rose For Emily (and other stories)*. The cover (see page 20) shows what you'd presume is the hardcover edition of the collection, which traditionally preceded the paperback reprint, but the hardcover shown is a dummy. My ASE is a true first edition first printing of Faulkner's first work.

My copy also has what's called a 'point,' signifying some kind of publisher's error. Opposite the Faulkner title page is a map from the next title in the ASE series, a fictional mystery. The question is whether ASE would bother to fix a mistake in a book that was never sold but simply given away. An examination of subsequent ASE printings reveals they did!

I'm reminded now of another one-of-a-kind experiment. Pocket Books, the first American mass-market paperback publisher, published Victor Hugo's massive novel, *The Hunchback of Notre Dame,* in 1939. It was their thirty-first title. Pocket established the retail paperback price at twenty-five cents, which the entire publishing industry replicated and stayed with until 1953, when most paper imprints shifted to thirty-five cents so longer novels would be possible without abridging. No one wanted to abridge anything in the first years.

In 1939, Pocket decided they couldn't publish a novel this long and make any profit, so they released *Hunchback* in two separate twenty-five-cent novels, as #31 and #32, and asked retailers to display them together. This was difficult, as "spinner racks" didn't yet exist in drugstores, cigar stores, stationery shops, and bus stations—the primary retail points-of-purchase.

Pocket also published Alexander Dumas' *The Three Musketeers*, another very long read, as two separate volumes. When Pocket yielded to the impulse to issue *Anna Karenina* as a movie tie-in in 1948, picturing Vivian Leigh and Kieran Moore on the cover, they did abridge—noting on the cover, "this edition has been specially prepared to make it shorter and more easily read." Pocket was the Cadillac of the industry, and their awkwardly worded decision opened the gates to abridgments right and left, before the price went to thirty-five cents industrywide, five years later.

You can understand why including "complete and unabridged" on the cover was so important in reassuring consumers that a pocket-size paperback at a quarter had exactly the same content as a jacketed hardcover, commonly priced at $2.00 in proper bookstores.

A lot of factors work against the sidewalk vendor, starting with the weather. It's too cold or too hot,or too windy or too rainy. Most merchants would rather not have competition twenty feet from their front door, which the local law permits. Dogs think the table is a tree, birds drop their loads on my hat and my tablecloth, cars drive up on sidewalks trying to park, streets get closed off for parades or fires or floods. Finding a bathroom without a line or a coded lock is difficult. Crazy people walk up and just stare at the books. People don't understand why I don't have a business card, why I don't take credit cards, why I don't do anything online other than email. I don't carry or own a mobile device of any kind, by design. I tell customers to look at the table as a one-day pop-up shop, because I may not have the strength to lug this mountain out next weekend. I think I'm customer-friendly, but I'm not customer-cooperative. The notion of going through all this to maybe put a few extra steaks in the freezer is, by almost any criterion, absurd. I could make far more as a senior greeter at Wendy's—and with benefits.

But the attraction of curating one table for 8 million people is irresistible. The conversations can be delicious, and they happen spontaneously. Philip Roth and I once discussed why his paperback editions won't be worth anything until a half-century after he's dead, because the printings were so large. James Levine, David Halberstam, Martha Plimpton, Whoopi Goldberg, and Damon Wayans have all been customers. Richard Holbrooke used to stop with his United Nations security staff while he purchased gifts for his UN colleagues. Former Avon publisher Michael Morrison Knopf's late CEO, Sonny Mehta, and the late *Black Enterprise* publisher, Earl Graves, have browsed and bought. I took requested titles up to the late Ian Ballantine, who founded early and important imprints, and "walked his shelves," picking titles in trade.

I've had hundreds of street encounters over the years of Saturdays and Sundays at my table of pulps. Some have left lasting impressions. One of my first brief conversations with a boldface name was with Gregory Corso, the Beat writer. He bounced around and hopped up and down, decrying his outrage that a paperback costing a quarter was priced at $50 on the street. I couldn't tell if he was half-kidding or dead serious. Maybe the former, because he finally slapped me on the back, advised me to carry on the bookman's trade, and vaulted away. Those who knew Corso confirm that he was a piece of work.

My one visit with a major cover artist was a late
'80s conversation with Leo Manso, who spotted
his archetypal hardboiled painting on a first Pocket
printing of *The Glass Key* and introduced himself. He
told me he'd earned $75 for painting it in 1943 and
had saved few of his paperback paintings. Manso
was a fine artist whose works are in the permanent
collections of the Museum of Modern Art and the
Metropolitan Museum. In the '40s he briefly formed
a guild with illustrator George Salter dedicated to
upgrading paperback art. Robert Motherwell could

have been referring directly to the Hammett *Glass Key* cover when he said, "Seductively beautiful as Manso's work is at first light, it holds its own like iron, a visual poetry that never compromises, never loses its inner life."

I set up one afternoon in front of a theater where Raymond Carver was reading that night, figuring that would draw a literary crowd. Sure enough, Ray and his companion, Tess Gallagher, walked up. I said, "You're too young for this table," and avowed there were no minimalists here, knowing he disliked being described as one. I think I called him "a dirty realist," which I'd read he liked, and he smiled. He smiled more when I told him I hoped he'd write a novel as long as Willard Motley's *Knock On Any Door* or *Down All Your Streets.* To my surprise he knew Motley's work, and we mostly talked about Chicago proletarian writers of the '30s.

Joey Adams wrote a cute '40s showbiz novel called
The Curtain Never Falls in which one character is
named Jackie Mason. The story is about a Broadway
comedian who achieved top billing professionally
and is ranked as a heel, humanly. Mason, the old
New York Jewish comedian himself, walks up to my
table one day and I figure I've got a sure sale. "Mr.
Mason, is the Jackie Mason character based on you?"
I ask, holding up my copy of *The Curtain Never Falls*.
He stares long and hard at the book and the back
blurb referencing 'Jackie Mason.' "No, it's not me,"
he says, puts down the book and starts to walk away.
"Are you sure?" I cry desperately. He turns back to
me: "If it was me, I'd know, and I'd buy the book,"
he replies. I subsequently looked up the book review
in the October 8, 1949, edition of the entertainment
newspaper *Billboard*. "Whether Mason is a replica of
any single comic now around, or a combination of
several comics, is a question that should cause plenty
of speculation." So we are still guessing. In any case,

the real guy's famous line resonates personally with me now. "I have enough money to last me the rest of my life unless I buy something."

Some years ago Jay Cocks, who used to be *Time*'s film critic and now writes screenplays for Marty Scorsese (*Silence, Gangs of New York, The Age of Innocence*), asked if I had a recommendation for a birthday gift for the esteemed director. We inventoried the table and decided on William Lindsay Gresham's *Nightmare Alley*, to which movie star Tyrone Power had bought the rights because he wanted to play a carny hustler who bites the heads off chickens—instead of the handsome, cardboard leading man he'd become. The paperback is a snazzy Signet edition with Avati's art of a carny cutie who doesn't look much like either Joan Blondell or Coleen Gray, and nothing like Helen Walker, the bad-girl Park Avenue psychiatrist.

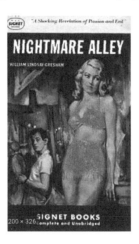

Jay reported several weeks later that Marty was so pleased with the novel that "it's on his shortlist for a future remake."

An older woman with some mileage on her came up one day and thumbed through every title propped up in my '30s open suitcase. She picked out a 1951 Bantam copy of *Model Railroading* with a Lionel model locomotive rocketing down the rails on the front cover.

I have no idea why I even had the book on the table, except that I liked the vivid cover art.

"That's the one," she said, paying me. "Are you a model railroad-train fan?" I asked cautiously, because she hardly looked like one. "My man is; he bought the company," she replied. I paused...then tried "Are you Neil Young's wife?" "I certainly am," she replied, and gave me a hug. "This will make Neil's day," she grinned. He was doing shows up the street. The next weekend she came back and said Neil was thrilled to have the book.

I've had Madonna at the table, not once but twice, and didn't recognize her in her elaborate disguise (hat, huge sunglasses, big scarf, slouched-over posture). She hummed away both times and didn't buy anything, but immediately after she wandered off, people flocked up—from Lord knows where? doorways? windows?—and said "Didn't you know that was Madonna?" Of course I hadn't a clue.

If I had to do a table of a hundred titles and could pick only one book to offer, it would be J.D. Salinger's *Catcher in the Rye* with Jim Avati's cover. Avati, who hailed from Red Bank, New Jersey, was Signet's premiere cover artist in the '50s, had sat down with Salinger, who didn't want a cover painting at all. Avati advised him if he wanted to sell any books in paper, he absolutely needed his artistic eye. Salinger considered that and told Avati he could live with a painting of Holden Caulfield, from the back, looking at the carousel in Central Park. "That's a terrible idea," responded Avati. He advised Salinger he'd paint a portrait of Holden marching down Broadway with his Gladstone luggage, wearing his hunting cap on backwards, thinking about all the movies he was going to see and hate that day. "That's a worse idea," replied Salinger, but he endured over twenty printings of *Catcher* with the Broadway painting and finally ordered Signet to scrub all visuals from his paperback reprints. The carousel scenario eventually ended up on a British reprint.

James Avati was fond of telling people who asked how he could have knocked out so many paintings, one after another after another, for Signet in the '50s, that he "got the faces right, and cheated a lot on the backgrounds." There's truth in this: the faces are vivid—he used a palette knife to chisel out grooves around eyes and noses and mouths, so the facial detail would stay sharp on the canvas when it came down twenty times in size. As much as anything else, that's what makes Avati covers so distinct. Thus some of his big oils look a touch grotesque and have to be carefully lighted when they're displayed. You know the girl in Dreiser's *An American Tragedy* cover is pregnant, not because she's showing but by the look in her eyes as she stares at herself in her bedroom mirror, one hand casually placed on her stomach.

You get hunches about certain books or even certain cover art, because you never know whom they'll attract. I've sold more than one copy of Al Capp's *The Schmoo* to women who've called their husband by that name all their married lives. I had a movie tie-in British hardcover in paperback size of *The Singing Fool* with Al Jolson pictured on the cover. It would have made a nice item for Rod Stewart when he swaggered up, but I couldn't take my eyes off the beguiling gal he had on his arm, and never remembered to show him the book.

You need to understand that time is working against the table. Authors who were slightly familiar in the '80s when I ventured out with this hobby have fast faded from most memories. Younger readers know classic authors only from the movies made from their books, like the Bond novels, *To Kill a Mockingbird,* and *Breakfast at Tiffany's.*

Movie companies used to advertise the book to promote their movies, like *Leave Her to Heaven* and Spillane's *I, The Jury.* They rarely do that today. My favorite film of the last few years out of hundreds viewed and dozens reviewed for *The Independent* (*Independent-magazine.org*) was Todd Haynes' *Wonderstruck,* from Brian Selznick's young-readers' novel. The film didn't last long in several Manhattan art cinemas that rarely attract families to anything, a missed opportunity in not promoting Selznick's magical book or his equally quicksilver novel that became Scorsese's *Hugo.*

The one title that seems to have stayed with the

same cover art forever is James Hilton's *Lost Horizon*,
painted by Isador Steinberg.

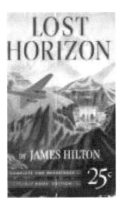

Maybe there's a universal longing in everyone who
reads and recommends the novel for the mysterious
lost world of *Shangri-La*, captured so vividly by Steinberg in 1939. Pocket Books recognized this, making
it their first title after getting good buzz on their tiny
Good Earth test printing. The grandchildren of Steinberg have introduced themselves at my book table,
but alas, their granddad never saved his fabulous
Pocket cover paintings. Very few illustrators of the
era did, but James Avati saved them all and got some
handsome paydays in his twilight years, as most of

his original oils sold in the $5,000–$15,000 range. I could have bought Avati's original cover of *Catcher In The Rye* for $6,000 twenty years ago, but passed because Avati later painted over a chunk of his painting onto which Signet had surprinted a selling blurb that both he and Salinger hated through the years. The general opinion was the white paint was embedded permanently, and I thought *this is just too weird to spend the rest of my life explaining away.* (I shoulda bought it anyway.) Avati fans will want to order a copy of *The Paperback Art of James Avati* (Piet Schreuders and Kenneth Fulton; Donald Grant Publisher, 2005). Schreuders also authored *Paperbacks U.S.A., A Graphic History (1939–59),* and *Blue Dolphin,* (1981), which details the lives of all the major paperback illustrators and leads big-time with Avati and his work. In 1981, Schreuders staged a pioneering paperback art show at the Gemeente Museum in The Hague including works by Avati, Richard Powers, Charles Addams, Dell's Map Back ace Gerald Gregg, and Penguin's superb illustrator Robert Jonas.

The preface to the Schreuders's work on Avati is by Stanley Meltzoff, also a Signet illustrator and Jim's close friend. Meltzoff considered himself an Avati protégé and styled his own cover illustrations much like Avati's, as a tribute more than anything else. He organized the one major showing and sale of many of Jim's major Signet paintings here in Manhattan—that's where I saw and thought about *Catcher*. I have a couple of postcard flyers on that, signed by Avati. Meltzoff's take was that "Avati was the master—the rest of us just passed through," which shows the reverence he felt for Jim and his work. Most of Avati's Signet covers through the '50s used local Red Bank residents. Jim's daughter turns up over and over, as do a number of his neighbors. The two Signets with the largest number of neighbors are probably Ralph Ellison's *Invisible Man* (a Signet double-volume twin-spine fifty-center) and Thomas Merton's *The Seven Storey Mountain*, with a variety of souls clustered in a cave.

I have an extremely rare video, *James Avati—King of Bookcovers*, which was released on VHS only in 2000 by Kulture Video, then located in West Long Branch, New Jersey. Its copyright is VPRO Television, The Netherlands. It runs fifty-five minutes and is extraordinarily revealing and interesting, showing Avati at work and moseying around Red Bank.

The cover art on countless paperbacks stays with us long after we've forgotten much of the book. Everyone my age—born in 1938—remembers Irving Shulman's *The Amboy Dukes*, with its cool Brooklyn couple, played in the movie *City Across The River* by Tony Curtis and Julie Adams, because it was the first coming-of-age novel teens read under the covers with a flashlight, looking to see if some Amboy Street bonehead dopester would get the second button of Betty's blouse undone. Are you surprised Ted Nugent named his first garage band after The Amboy Dukes?

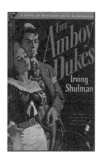

A bit more about Irving Shulman, because he was an industry. His first three sequential novels—*The Amboy Dukes, Cry Tough,* and *The Big Brokers*—trace a New York gang and whoever wasn't jailed or slain out to Las Vegas. James T. Farrell's *Studs Lonigan* trilogy and Danny O'Neill's quartet (*No Star is Lost, Fathers and Sons, My Days of Anger,* and *A World I Never Made*) were emblematic of Chicago youth, and don't have a fraction of the Dukes' staying power among old Manhattan denizens, female as well as male. Shulman then penned *Children of the Night,* which became the seminal James Dean film *Rebel Without A Cause.* Finally, he novelized the movie version of *West Side Story* that sold a zillion copies. Juvenile delinquency has its place in a *noir* town.

Maybe that's another reason why James Avati's iconic image of a loner kid roaming New York City's streets resonates so well with continuing generations.

Science fiction and fantasy used to sell better on the table than they do these days. Manhattan's several science-fiction/fantasy bookstores are gone—along with other specialty bookshops like The Military Bookman, Black Books Plus, The Oscar Wilde, Eeyore's, and The Complete Traveler, whose names defined their genres. Richard Belzer, the comedian, used to buy every UFO-related book I put on the table—people tell me he has the premiere "saucer" book collection in town. L. Ron Hubbard novels and pulp magazines with his stories are big, as you'd expect, with Scientologists.

The obsessive fans keep turning up. There's a dapper black guy on a fancy bike who rides around weekends with Edith Piaf songs—and that's all— playing out of a Pignose speaker attached to his bike seat, and he likes French authors. One dad I've gotten to know named his first son Dashiell and is slowly building a collection of Dashiell Hammett paperbacks of hard-boiled detective stories. There are members of the Wolfe Pack literary society who naturally want to see any of Rex Stout's *Nero Wolfe* titles, and David Goodis fans who save up for their annual trek down to Philadelphia for a pub crawl around the bars that Goodis frequented and set his novels of sorry-ass losers in.

Twenty years ago lesbian couples would shyly walk up. I'd wait to see if they were interested in the genre—some are, some aren't—and usually they'd start the conversation asking about some fairly obscure lesbian writer like Valerie Taylor or Kimberly Kemp. They were testing me, curious whether I really knew anything about their bookshelves.

Today, female couples bluster up and just blurt out, "Okay, where's your queer pulps?" And I start dishing out the Ann Bannon titles I have; she is the queen of lesbian pulp fiction. Or Marijane Meaker, who also wrote under the names Vin Packer, M.E. Kerr, and Ann Aldrich. I also occasionally point out there was never a same-sex pulp story in the history of the pulp-magazine industry. Maybe the table has made an impression on Broadway—or more likely not, but the culture is far, far more open. Titles like *Nigger Heaven* by Carl Van Vechten and *Twelve Chinks and a Woman* by James Hadley Chase raise eyebrows today, but they have a cultural relevance, and I offer them as the rare collectibles they've become.

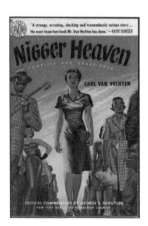

One paperback I always enjoy talking about is the 1952 first Avon printing of Aldous Huxley's *After Many a Summer Dies the Swan*.

The tale I'm relating here has been passed down to me, with varying details, by book and movie people for years, and I think much of it, maybe most of it, is true: In 1939 Orson Welles and producer John Houseman were laboring away at MGM, when the Huxley novel—a biographical tale loosely based on media tycoon William Randolph Hearst—was published. It was less than flattering, and Welles watched carefully to see if Hearst would refute or protest the book, but Hearst stayed silent. Welles took that as a signal to proceed with his screenplay of

Citizen Kane in which Welles himself would portray the Hearst-like media superman Charles Foster Kane. Hearst heard about Welles's filming and was intensely curious to see a print, so he bribed an editor at RKO Pictures, which was producing the film, to let him watch a copy. What he saw and heard infuriated him, but not for reasons you might imagine. In the movie, Kane has a childhood sled called Rosebud. It's become a universal symbol of everyone's childhood, and has even turned up in an Absolut vodka ad. At the time, Hearst, who was married, had sequestered a gal pal, the well-known silent-screen actress Marion Davies, in a Malibu hideaway. Welles had somehow discovered that Hearst's pet name for Miss Davies's most private body part was "rosebud." Hearst stormed into RKO's offices and demanded the negative of *Citizen Kane*, offering a million dollars and claiming he'd be ruined if the movie was released.

The story goes that both RKO and Welles briefly considered Hearst's offer, as the movie had cost $600,000 to produce, but decided the world should see it. Hearst was furious and tried to block the picture's New York premiere, but Henry Luce, at *Time* magazine, had also heard the story and weighed in, gleefully backing its showing. The picture opened to poor reviews and even weaker business, probably because people were used to hearing Welles's Mercury Theater radio players—the major supporting actors in *Citizen Kane*—in all the popular radio programs America listened to—everything from *The Shadow* to Welles' famous *War of the Worlds* broadcast in 1938. So why should people lay out good money to see the same radio gang they listened to at home for free?

Citizen Kane languished for years until the world slowly came to perceive its innovative and artistic excellence as, well, maybe the best American movie ever. Do you know what happened to the Rosebud sled? Steven Spielberg apparently bought it at auction in 1983 for $55,000. When I tell this story, and I've told it more than once because I've had the paperback more than once, the copy of the book usually goes home with the listener. Sharing the stories is a great part of the value of the object.

In my more than three decades of selling on New York City sidewalks, no one has ever stolen a paperback. This may be as good as an indication as any that thieves regard a sidewalk book table of old paperbacks with indifference at best. I did lose one pulp magazine, years ago, to a bike messenger who whizzed by and grabbed a pulp out of a back suitcase rack, probably thinking it was a comic book. To my knowledge, no one has ever led a comparative study on theft statistics per literary genre.

On the other hand, I've watched dumbstruck as a $900 sports bike disappeared in fifteen seconds from a light pole ten feet away from me that a young Wall Street type had fastened with a massive chain and a heavy-duty lock. One small exception: I didn't see it happen, but the NYPD that investigated the owner's frantic 911 call inspected the lock and said it looked like it had been dissolved by liquid nitrogen—apparently the same "freezing" chemical that dermatologists use to "mist off" spots on one's face only in deadly concentrated form. He said it probably took fifteen seconds for a thief wearing gloves, carefully tilting a vial of the chemical, to burn through the lock. The things you pick up on the street.

Sitting beside a book table on a summer day in Lincoln Center from 8:00 a.m. to 8:00 p.m. requires enormous patience and a certain degree of detachment. If 50,000 people walk by in twelve hours—a modest estimate—95 percent will totally ignore the table. Because the area is an end-destination for people attending an opera, ballet, play, or film, most passersby have never seen the table, but many subconsciously register it as a table of books or possibly CDs. The pulp magazines are initially perceived by almost everyone as comic books. Half the people who do walk up are tourists looking for Lincoln Center or Broadway or a bathroom. And I tell them they're standing in Lincoln Center, on Broadway, with directions to a bathroom. Some folks still look for Barnes & Noble, which had a multi-story branch that shut down several years ago. The day can be more than a little discouraging.

Generally, I sit on my folding stool, take an old paperback from its polybag sleeve, and lose myself in a novel; this helps identify the product and also demonstrates that seventy-five-year-old paperbacks are quite readable. Some people wandering up are genuinely curious. Only a fraction instantly register what they're looking *at*, and, once in a blue moon, even looking *for*. New York is indeed a city of 8 million stories, and I've never been able to correctly identify a certain kind of reader by age, ethnicity, gender, dress, or demeanor, so everyone starts out on a level playing field. Fewer and fewer people carry cash, but as you'd expect in one of New York City's most tony and expensive neighborhoods, there are four banks with open ATMs in my sightline or within a block.

Packing up in the rain is the paperback guy's worst nightmare. I usually don't set up if there's a 30 percent chance or more of rain. Broadway around Lincoln Center is a wind tunnel, because the avenue is extremely wide and opens to a large plaza and fountain. Gray clouds and light breezes can turn into black skies and gusty winds in a New York minute. Paperbacks have no weight—a 30 mph gust can tip the book table over into the street in seconds. This has happened more than once. Suddenly I'm chasing books and my hat down Broadway—and then it starts to pour.

I've built a lot of my knowledge about old paperbacks from a small band of rabid collectors who know imprints, authors, plots, and cover artists like the backs of their hands. For a quarter century Gary Lovisi and his wife Lucille ran an annual paperback show at a West 57th street hotel. Gary's a publisher, writer and lifelong collector of this stuff, and he's probably never happier than when he's poking around some dusty attic with a flashlight at an estate sale, looking to unearth some gem.

Until his passing, Jon White was Manhattan's premiere collector for decades, and presided over a floor-to-ceiling room filled with paper and pulp in a Chelsea warehouse, where he was a "completist" through the '40s and '50s on a lot of imprints. Tom Lesser and Rose Islet have run the California annual rare paper and pulp shows out of Glendale for decades, and have invaluable knowledge they freely share. More than anyone, Rose at her Black Ace Books deepened me into the hobby and the notion of trying to sell vintage paperbacks when I was flying in and out of LA to shoot commercials in the '80s.

Robert Polito, who ran the writing program at The New School for decades and authored the Jim Thompson bio *Savage Art*, supported my "Pulp Fiction" and "Killer Writers" humanities courses there for years, both of which dug deep into vintage paper. Geoffrey O'Brien, editor-in-chief at the Library of America, guested classes on David Goodis, and in fact introduced New School students to Thompson and Goodis long before anyone else. The late crime maestro Donald E. Westlake also visited the writers' class, and shared chapter and verse with me (though not the students) on his salad days pumping out sleaze novels and fiery lesbian romances under names like Edwin West to pay the rent.

A Lion Books author (*Sinners' Game*, 1954), Linton Baldwin became a close personal friend through his twilight years. He'd taken my New School lit courses, but outside the classroom, Linton became a mentor who was an unabashed cheerleader for the table. Baldwin's one novel is a boxing yarn featuring a gal named Rain who wears a white raincoat and has too much past and too little future.

The editor of Lion, Arnold Hano, gave Baldwin the cover painting because the artist had painted it for another pulpy Lion manuscript that was never finished. Baldwin and Hano agreed it worked fine for *Sinners' Game*. So do I. Lion's paperback art, like so many pulp covers, has an "emotional urgency" that a major pulp editor in the '30s once demanded of cover artists. On a spinner rack in a Greyhound bus station in Memphis in 1954, it communicated instantly. It's timeless because its emotional urgency is forever. You wouldn't want the lug in the doorway to cover this "TNT blonde"—oh wait, she's a redhead here—with a white raincoat, would you?

I suppose I've learned how literature migrates onto the screen more closely through my teaching of crime novels and *film noir*. For the past fifteen years, at The 92nd Street Y, I've taught the course "Killer Movies: Lost Films Noir." We've rarely shown the same film twice, and I keep trying to whittle down a basic definition of the genre into one still. This is my forever favorite:

It's from Universal's 1944 *Phantom Lady*, based on the 1942 novel by Cornell Woolrich, who lived with his mother in the Hotel Marseilles at Broadway and 103rd until her passing in 1957. Woolrich was Manhattan's premiere *noir* novelist and short-story pulpster, and many of his stories and novels (some written under his pseudonyms William Irish and George Hopley) have become indelible crime/suspense movies: *The Bride Wore Black, Rear Window, Deadline at Dawn, No Man Of Her Own, I Married A Dead Man, The Black Angel, Night Has A Thousand Eyes.*

In *Phantom Lady,* Ella Raines is standing on the platform of the El train at Times Square, waiting for a 4:00 a.m. downtown train to her rooming house off 23rd Street. She's trying to track down whoever killed the wife of her employer, who's been tried and found guilty of a crime he didn't commit. The guy behind Ella, who's thinking about pushing her into the path of an approaching train, tends bar in a watering hole off Times Square where she's been sitting all night watching him. He's followed her onto the El platform. He's not the killer, but he's webbed into whoever is— though in a few minutes he'll be struck and killed by a passing car outside her building.

Innocents who make one fatal mistake, odd coincidences, and impossible plotting fill Woolrich's work, but it rarely matters, because at his best Woolrich concocted what he called "the line of suspense" that transcended logic and plausibility.

So does this film, so does this scene, and so does this particular moment and still. Raines and the actor are on a studio set. The cityscape above them, which also stretches down the tracks, is a painting that's been matted into the scene. The platform ceiling and the opposite platform, even the signal light and tracks, appear to be excellent miniatures. This is a stunning example of bipacking or even tripacking—fancy names for cut-and-paste—which were common in '40s cliffhanger serials. The defining image is on-screen no more than five seconds. Keep in mind this is half a century before computer-generated imagery (CGI).

The setting is claustrophobic, because it's tight, closed-in, completely artificial. The director, Robert Siodmak, was a German emigré well acquainted with the expressionism that first defined *film noir* with its meager sets and chiaroscuro lighting. You're watching an illusion far more tense and frightening than real-life location photography could ever achieve. This is *film noir*.

It's not surprising that my favorite crime writer— both on the table and in my own *films noir* course at The 92nd Street Y—is Raymond Chandler. Though he wrote only two dozen short stories and seven novels, Chandler was clearly the most important literary crime pulpster and novelist of the 20th century; everyone else sort of passed through. Nearly all Chandler's novels started out as pulp stories in either *Black Mask* or *Dime Detective*, where he experimented with several private eyes who would coalesce into Philip Marlowe.

The 1939 issue shown of *Dime Detective*, which was a more lurid and bizarre pulp than *Black Mask*, uses the familiar skeleton/skull motif, a semiotic signal to people walking past a street newsstand or a bus station magazine rack that this is a mystery magazine. Skulls and skeletons pop up on hundreds of pulp and paperback covers in the '30s and '40s.

The dentist drilling away on the skull's bony teeth is a tribute of sorts to the Grand Guignol, which was the longest-running theater of prosthetics and torture devices in the world. New York's pulp publishers traveled to the Guignol's vest-pocket Paris theater in the '30s to view its dynamite format—a half-hour grisly play, with an intermission with smelling salts and nurses in attendance, then another half-hour playlet, this time a comedy, featuring the same restored cast. What a nifty concept. The publishers quickly launched a line of "weird menace" horror and terror pulps, which were eventually shut down by New York's shocked mayor, Fiorello La Guardia. *Dime Detective* softened its imagery and was able to continue through the '40s.

You can tell Chandler was finding his way in 1939, because a piece of *Lady in the Lake* is included in this issue, and he just barely made it onto the cover in its lower left corner. The lead story is by Erle Stanley Gardner, a better-known pulpster who would eventually become the world-famous creator of Perry Mason and female private eye Bertha Cool.

Chandler's crowning achievement, *The Big Sleep*, deserves more detailed examination. The novel was cobbled together by Chandler from two *Black Mask* stories, "Killer in the Rain" (1935) and "The Curtain" (1936). Chapters 4, 6–10, and 12–16 derive from the earlier pulp story, and chapters 1–3, 20, and 27–32 from the latter. The novel's other eleven chapters are new material that expand, collapse, and stitch together the two stories. Sort of.

It gets more complicated. Director Howard Hawks loved the book and hired Faulkner and Brackett to adapt it. Neither knew the other. Even Hawks assumed Brackett was a male from her hard-boiled crime fiction, but delighted in discovering she was an attractive, razor-sharp, and collegial woman. Faulkner, who had no experience in shaping crime fiction for the screen, was appalled to be partnered with a woman, so the two writers worked in adjacent bungalows in a Beverly Hills hotel on alternate chapters, rarely collaborating. Along with *The Big Sleep*'s cast and crew, Hawks was often puzzled by the frazzled continuity of Brackett and Faulkner's script. Initial filming was completed in January 1945.

Wait—things are about to get really confused. *The Big Sleep* found itself stuck in Warner's releasing pipeline as the studio, knowing the war was ending, rushed to open a slew of World War II themed films. Bogart and nineteen-year-old Lauren Bacall had been an instant hit with audiences in *To Have and Have Not*, two years earlier. Then Bacall went on to make *Confidential Agent* with Charles Boyer and received mostly negative notices. Bacall's agent, Charles K. Feldman, later a major producer, had a "big idea." Feldman wrote Jack Warner that *The Big Sleep* would have far greater appeal if Bacall and Bogart's scenes were reshot to enhance both her looks and their attraction. Feldman and Warner knew they had started an affair and would probably marry once Bogart divorced his wife. Warner agreed and ordered whole sets rebuilt to original specs, tasked Hawks, his cast, crew, and writers to return over a year later in early 1946, and reshot nine scenes punching up Lauren Bacall's wardrobe and deepening her onscreen relationship with Bogart. Various characters were changed and some were eliminated altogether, and the story became even more murky to follow. *The Big Sleep* was released in its slicked-up version in August 1946. That's the version we've watched most of our lives.

If you look at scene-by-scene comparisons of the original cut and the new version—which were compiled by UCLA film preservationist Robert Gitt and have been televised on Turner Classic Movies— you see a star being born and an already unglued story becoming virtually impossible to navigate. The story didn't matter. What counted was the *noir* chemistry between a worn, grizzled private eye and an exquisite young ingénue, truly falling in love before your eyes. *The Big Sleep* was a big hit, for which Jack Warner took full credit.

And then there's my own home reading. I try to alternate a '40s novel or author with a contemporary writer. Alice Munro is a favorite, in part because her Canadian tales seem to replicate my own childhood memories of spare Iowa towns and endless Wisconsin farmland, and in part because Munro has an uncanny gift for being able to seamlessly shift the narrative flow, abandoning one character to pick up the journey of another. Ditto James Salter, who had a priceless gift of being able to dissect marriages with the same precision as his descriptions of fearsome aerial combat. At the moment, I'm taking a turn through pulp magazines that even before the outbreak of World War II threw up cautionary tales about Japanese invaders and neo-Nazi brownshirts hovering around LA and Manhattan. I'm pairing those pulp tales with early wartime novels like

Sinclair Lewis's *It Can't Happen Here* and Lewis Browne's *See What I Mean?* that had the same Fifth Column focus. The past is prelude to the present, as they say.

Browsers occasionally ask me how I can bear to part with what is in part my original childhood reading. I've come to regard selling off the collection as another natural coming-of-life, or more accurately, going-of-life, passage. Not unlike overcoming a fear of the water or pedaling off on a bike or even flying for the first time—once you've learned these mysteries, trading off childhood memories for money isn't so daunting, especially books you're not dying to keep.   And occasionally I've actually replaced a book I've sold that I've found I miss too much: *Phantom of the Opera* was the last one. It didn't leave much of a space on a shelf, but my heart was lonely for it, though I couldn't tell you why.

Besides Philip Roth and Donald Westlake, the one world-renowned author I certainly recall encountering by chance, but this time in a bookstore, was Harper Lee, who created the beloved *To Kill A Mockingbird*. This occurred when two of my daughters were young and both attending a girls' school in my Upper East Side neighborhood. Late one morning, I had walked down the steps to the Bryn Mawr bookshop, which until its demise occupied a tiny basement space off 79th and York Avenue. Aside from the manager, Deb, the only person browsing shelves was Lee, and I was sure I recognized her at once, though I had no idea she maintained a one-bedroom apartment just four blocks north.

I was frozen. The first thing I did was casually check the fiction shelves and paperback section to see if there might be a copy of *Mockingbird*. Damn, not a one. I thought about sprinting home and running back with my copy, but decided she'd be gone, so

I moseyed over and quietly said, "Miss Lee?" She looked up with a half smile. "I just wanted to thank you for your wonderful book, and the movie it made," I blurted out. She was gracious and said she'd liked the film very much. I was literally tongue-tied but managed to get out that she should come talk to the girls at my daughters' school.

"Oh, no, they're much too bright for me," she murmured. That struck me as hilarious, but she added that they'd invited her more than once and she'd politely declined. I decided I'd worn out my welcome and backed off, but it was a serendipity kind of moment.

As a half-hearted retail merchant who doesn't seem to have too much skin in the game, I've turned down interview and feature-story requests from every daily newspaper and tabloid in the city. The reporter chemistry has never felt right. And part of my mentality clings to the anonymity most New Yorkers carry around and many actually relish, perhaps like Harper Lee could succeed at in Manhattan but not in her home town of Monroeville, Alabama.

But I've given two Q&A interviews to literary specialists. The first was a small Brooklyn literary magazine, *Explosion Proof*, and what won me over wasn't the insistence of the young women who ran it, but their promise that they'd run the interview in the same 2011 issue as their interview with novelist Mona Simpson. Sharing space with Simpson was a wowzer, a real confidence-builder.

The second occurred when a rare-book dealer from Bainbridge Island, Ed Smith, walked up and started marveling at the reality of a high-end vintage paperback table just several feet away from Broadway traffic. As an officer of the Antiquarian Booksellers' Association of America, Ed offered to shoot and post a spontaneous and unrehearsed interview on the ABAA website, and I said, "Start rolling." It has worked out fine, has pulled a couple thousand hits, and is worlds shorter than this gasbag narrative.

A day or two before Christmas may be the one time of the year when my book table works as a last-minute gift source. It's usually way too cold or windy to even try to set up in late December, but when New York's temps climb to 40 degrees Fahrenheit, which is only 5 degrees for the rest of the world, with no precipitation and no wind tunnel on Broadway, I throw on half the clothes I own and set it all up. The table does manage to help "put a few steaks in the freezer," as I occasionally tell people who wonder why this elderly chap is huddled over on a stool behind a table of '40s pulp and paperback rarities. Woody Allen would say we "do it for the eggs." This can't be mercantile. The merchant in front of me may even bring me a cup of hot tea and graciously invite me to warm up in his or her entrance and use the bathroom. That's what I call a swell day.

After all these years I consider myself a paid-in-full member of "the Broadway beat" that illustrator Ray Johnson painted for the 1951 Avon edition of columnist Louis Sobol's memoir of covering the "Gay White Way." Avon's back-cover blurb promises "The Low-Down on the High Hats and The Highlights on the Low-Lifes," which is a decent-enough definition of what New Yorkers take home as stocking stuffers, serious gifts, or additions to a bookshelf of favorite titles by a favorite author.

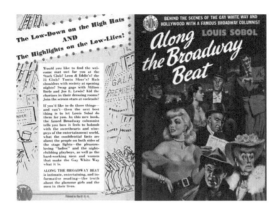

My editor and publisher, David Applefield, discovered these mini-treasures and me on a warmer, sunnier day. I keep thinking of the indelible Manhattan novels and pulp tales that Cornell Woolrich pounded out on a Remington portable typewriter in a residential hotel room overlooking Broadway in 1940. I'd like to think Woolrich and I make our way *Along The Broadway Beat* together, and that this season and next I'm the paperback guy keeping his high hats and low lives in the churn.

⌘

If I had to add an epilogue to this tale, there's one book-table story I've been reluctant to share but now somehow feel right doing so here. It's about the occasional meet-ups I had with Joe Mitchell, the legendary author and *New Yorker* staff writer for fifty-eight years. Mitchell died in 1996, and during his final years was confined to a wheelchair, under the care of his companion and literary executor, Sheila McGrath, a lovely woman. They lived a short walk from Zabar's at 80th and Broadway, and on a nice Saturday Sheila would wheel Joe up and he'd squint at all the paperbacks. He was always on the lookout for his own early collection of essays and interviews, *McSorley's Wonderful Saloon*, published by Penguin in paper in 1945.

As it happened, through the '80s and '90s, which were among my heavy drinking decades, I'd squirrel away copies of Mitchell's book, which I'd divide into little piles for one special day every few years. On that day, I'd take in three copies at 11:00 a.m., just as McSorley's down on 7th Street was unlocking its doors. There'd be three fresh-faced young Irish bartenders wiping down the bar for the day's business, and I'd get their undivided attention. "This is for you," I'd say, laying down a copy in front of the first guy. "Your job is to keep my scotch tumbler full through lunch and bring me a decent sandwich." I'd walk to the second fellow and lay down a copy for him. "You, young man, will keep my glass filled through the afternoon." And then the third: "And you, my fine friend, are my night man, and your job is to carry on their work and bring me your best house steak, medium well, with baked potato, around 7:00 p.m., and make sure I get into a proper cab home after dinner." They'd look at me and stare at the original books I was giving them, and one would always say, "Take a seat, sir," and I'd sit and drink and eat my way through a splendid day and evening at McSorley's—and never see a tab.

Joe Mitchell would listen to this story outside Zabar's again and again, and he'd laugh and bang his cane on the table and say, "You're all right, kid," or some such thing. After his passing, Sheila brought me hardcopies of *McSorley's Wonderful Saloon*, *Old Mr. Flood*, and *My Ears Are Bent*, which today have pride-of-place on my bookshelves. They're treasures, even though my days and nights at McSorley's wonderful saloon are long behind me.

About the Author

Kurt Brokaw, born in 1938 in Dubuque, Iowa, was Associate Teaching Professor at The New School for thirty-three years, taught film and literature at The 92nd Street Y, and is senior film critic of *The Independent* (*Independent-magazine.org*). He was a creative exec at four top-ten New York ad agencies, and creative director of RCA Records. His wife, Mona, and his four grown children—Leslie, Chris, Kate, and Tess—are all good readers. On nice weekends Kurt is often on Broadway in Lincoln Center or farther up Broadway by Zabar's with his table of paperbacks and pulp fiction. Browsers always welcome!

Photo by Greg Tolopko

David Applefield is a publishing and media specialist, editor, and writer. Born in Elizabeth, New Jersey, and a graduate of Amherst College and Northeastern University, Applefield has worked in France, the U.S., the UK, and across Africa. He lives in Red Bank, New Jersey, where he is running for U.S. Congress (NJ4). The **Kiwai Media** imprint is a values-based publishing house and media firm publishing and marketing ebooks, print-on-demand books, and trade titles by thought-leaders, storytellers, and inspiring individuals.

david@kiwaimedia.com

US Toll Free: (855) 707-2747

www.kiwaimedia.com

Illustration Credits

Orchard Street
Publisher: *New York Daily News*

Argosy, August 28, 1937
Artist: Rudolph Belarski
Publisher: Frank A. Munsey, 280 Broadway, New
    York City, London, and Paris (Hachette)

Cup of Gold
Artist: Rudolph Belarski
Popular Library, 1950

Startling Stories, March 1951
Artist: Earle Bergey
Better Publications, 10 East 40th, New York City,
    Editorial Offices

Gentlemen Prefer Blondes
Artist: Earle Bergey
Popular Library, 1950

Sucker Bait
Artist: Walter Popp
Publisher: Graphic Mystery, 1950

A Rose for Emily and Other Stories
Armed Services Edition, 1945
First edition, first printing

Tarzan and the Forbidden City
Publisher: Bantam, 1939

My Reminiscences as a Cowboy
Artist: Rockwell Kent
Publisher: Boni Books, 1930

The Good Earth
Artist: Isador Steinberg
Publisher: Pocket Books, 1938–39
Test printing

"Soldier Art"
Infantry Journal / Fighting Forces Series, 1945

The Hunchback of Notre Dame
Artist: Isador Steinberg
Publisher: Pocket Books, 1939

The Glass Key
Artist: Leo Manso
Publisher: Pocket Books, 1943

The Curtain Never Falls
Artist: Earle Bergey
Publisher: Popular Library, 1950

Nightmare Alley
Artist: James Avati
Publisher: Signet, 1949

Model Railroading
Artist Unknown
Publisher: Bantam Books, 1950

The Catcher in the Rye
Artist: James Avati
Publisher: Signet Books, 1953

Lost Horizon
Artist: Isador Steinberg
Publisher: Pocket Books, 1939

The Amboy Dukes
Artist: Ann Cantor
Publisher: Avon Books, 1949

Nigger Heaven
Artist Unknown
Publisher: Avon Books, 1951

Twelve Chinks and a Woman
Artist: Wes
Publisher: Harlequin, 1952

After Many a Summer Dies the Swan
Artist Unknown
Publisher: Avon Books, 1952

Sinners' Game
Artist Unknown (the original painting is owned by
author Linton Baldwin's widow)
Publisher: Lion Books, 1954

Scene from *Phantom Lady*
Studio: Universal Pictures, 1944

Dime Detective
Artist: Unknown
Popular Publications, 1939

The Big Sleep
Artist: Paul Stahr
Publisher: Avon Books, 1942

To Kill a Mockingbird
Publisher: Pocket Library, 1962

Along the Broadway Beat
Artist: Ray Johnson
Publisher: Avon Books, 1950

McSorley's Wonderful Saloon
Artist Unknown
Publisher: Penguin Books, 1945